To
Megan

From
Love Grandma
This will help you
UNDERSTAND Little boys.

Celebrate *the* Wonder of Little Boys

Snips & Snails

AND PUPPY DOG TAILS

CHRYS HOWARD

Bestselling author of HUGS FOR BROTHERS

HOWARD BOOKS
A DIVISION OF SIMON & SCHUSTER
New York London Toronto Sydney

HOWARD
BOOKS

Published by Howard Books, a division of Simon & Schuster, Inc.
1230 Avenue of the Americas, New York, NY 10020
www.howardpublishing.com

Library of Congress Cataloging-in-Publication Data is available.

ISBN-13: 978-1-4165-7914-4
ISBN-10:   1-4165-7914-1
1 3 5 7 9 10 8 6 4 2

Manufactured in China

For information regarding special discounts for bulk purchases, please contact:
Simon & Schuster Special Sales at 1-800-456-6798 or business@simonandschuster.com.

Cover and interior design by Left Coast Design, Inc., Portland, OR 97229

Time Out Ladies by Dale Evans Rogers (Grand Rapids, MI: Fleming Revell,
a division of Baker Publishing Group, 1975). Used with permission.

Scriptures quoted from *The Holy Bible, New Century Version,*
copyright © 1987, 1988, 1991 by Word Publishing, Dallas, Texas 75234. Used by permission.

To my brothers, Kevin, Kerry, and Jeremy–

who allowed me to take a glimpse into the world of boyhood

To my son, Ryan, and grandsons, John Luke,

Asa, Will, Maddox, and Aevin–

who let me continue the adventure

What are little boys made of?

What are little boys made of?

Frogs and snails

And puppy dog tails,

That's what little boys are made of.

What are little girls made of?

What are little girls made of?

Sugar and spice

And all things nice,

That's what little girls are made of.

ROBERT SOUTHEY

English poet, 1774–1843

What are little boys made of?

Snips and snails and
puppy dog tails

Daddies and cane poles
and sharing a fishing hole

Lizards and frogs and balancing on logs

God made a world out of his dreams,

Of wondrous mountains, oceans, and streams,

Prairies and plains and wooded land,

Then paused and thought, "I need someone to stand

On top of the mountains, to conquer the seas,

Explore the plains and climb the trees,

Someone to start small and grow

sturdy, strong like a tree."

He created boys, full of spirit and fun,

To explore and conquer, to romp and run,

With dirty faces, banged up chins,

With courageous hearts and boyish grins.

When He had completed the task He'd begun,

He said, "That's a job well done."

ART KNIGHT

Everything on earth, shout with joy to God!

Sing about his glory! Make his praise glorious!

PSALM 66:1–2

Boys are found everywhere–on top of, underneath, inside of,

climbing on, swinging from, running around, or jumping to.

Mothers love them, little girls hate them, older sisters and brothers

tolerate them, adults ignore them and Heaven protects them.

DALE EVANS ROGERS

What are little boys made of?

Adventure and delight
and campfires at night

Laughter and charm and trips to the farm

Let our sons in their youth grow like plants.

PSALM 144:12

I meant to do my work today—

But a brown bird sang in the apple tree,

And a butterfly flitted across the field,

And all the leaves were calling me.

And the wind went sighing over the land,

Tossing the grasses to and fro,

And a rainbow held out its shining hand—

So what could I do but laugh and go?

RICHARD LE GALLIENNE

There comes a time in every rightly constructed boy's life when

he has a raging desire to go somewhere and dig for hidden treasure.

MARK TWAIN
The Adventures of Tom Sawyer

What are little boys made of?

Bikes after school and
playing it cool

Fire trucks and hoses and freckles on noses

He has put his angels in charge of you

to watch over you wherever you go.

PSALM 91:11

I'm not really sure
What I might grow up to be.
But I know that God has my plans—
He's holding them for me.

He's molding and He's shaping,
And I can't wait to see
The kind of person I'll become
And what God has planned for me.

Does He see me in an office
Sending out a fax?
Or maybe at a shopping mall
Figuring the tax?

Does He see me in an airplane
Flying high up above?
Or maybe I'm a preacher man
Sharing of God's love?

I guess I have to wait and see—
It's not as if I mind—
I'll gladly let God guide my steps
And follow close behind.

CHRYS HOWARD

The childhood shows the man, as morning shows the day.

JOHN MILTON

Paradise Regained

What are little boys made of?

Helmets and hats and footballs and bats

Running and sliding and tangled colliding

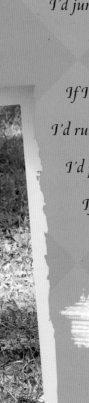

If I were very, very tall, as tall as I could be,

I'd play with all the little birds up in the topmost tree.

I'd jump right over houses and think nothing of a wall,

If I were very, very, very, very, very tall!

If I were very, very small, as small as I could be,

I'd run among the blades of grass where you could barely see;

I'd play with ants and beetles and I know I'd love them all.

If I were very, very, very, very, very small!

JOYCE L. BRISLEY

The heavens declare the glory of God, and the skies
announce what his hands have made.

PSALM 19:1

A child is a person who is going to carry on what you have started. . . . The fate of humanity is in his hands.

ABRAHAM LINCOLN

What are little boys made of?

Feathers and vests
and saving the west

Dragons and dinosaurs and guards for castle doors

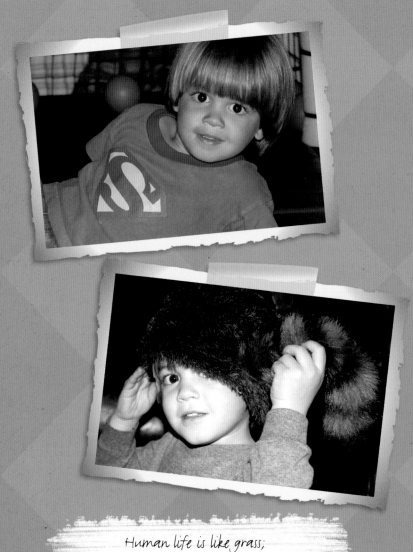

I'll get a rope and grab a hat

And put some boots on me,

Then I can be most anything

I could dream to be.

Even though it's make-believe,

It's fun just the same

To pretend for just a while;

I know it's just a game.

Yesterday I was Superman;

Today I'm Daniel Boone.

Tomorrow I will climb a tree

And fly up to the moon.

CHRYS HOWARD

Human life is like grass;

we grow like a flower in the field.

PSALM 103:15

Keep your eyes on the stars and your feet on the ground.

THEODORE ROOSEVELT

What are little boys made of?

Friendship and fun
and enjoying the sun

Wiggles and haircuts
and giggles and
funny looks

A child to hold and cuddle,

'Tis a gift from God above.

And the world is so much brighter,

When you have a child to love.

AUTHOR UNKNOWN

God makes the world all over again

whenever a little child is born.

JEAN PAUL RICHTER

I praise you because you made me

in an amazing and wonderful way.

What you have done is wonderful.

I know this very well.

PSALM 139:14

What are little boys made of?

Hugs and kisses and middle-of-the-night wishes

Toys and bears and sweet good-night prayers

That's what little boys are made of.

Each second we live is a new and unique moment

of the universe, a moment that will never be again...

And what do we teach our children?...

We should say to each of them: Do you know what you are?

You are a marvel. You are unique.

In all the years that have passed, there has never been another child like you.

Your legs, your arms, your clever fingers, the way you move.

You may become a Shakespeare, a Michelangelo, a Beethoven.

You have the capacity for anything. Yes, you are a marvel.

PABLO·CASALS